WELCOME

Contents

Worship matters.

I probably don't need to persuade you of that. You wouldn't have picked this pack up if you didn't share that belief. It matters because it's our response to all that God has done. Creation, salvation, consummation, the whole story begins with God. Our response, our worship is, at its most basic and best, the way we have discovered of saying 'Wow'. The implications for our whole lives are immense.

How we worship matters.

In asserting the significance of worship, I'm not, of course, referring to style or tradition. Rather I'm underlining the power of gathered worship, in all its forms, to shape us as disciples of Christ. This resource, and the book *Whole Life Worship* that it partners, spring from the conviction that our patterns of worship together on Sunday can profoundly re-shape us to live as disciples of Jesus, Monday to Saturday.

Some of you have long been persuaded about these possibilities. You may even have used LICC's resources, been on our training days, read our books and encouraged us with your own stories of fruitfulness. You'll know that we're excited about worship and church and God's people making a difference in their everyday lives. For others, this may be our first meeting, but you are committed to the renewal of worship in local churches and that has attracted you to this resource. We're so glad you've picked this up and joined us on this journey.

What we do in worship matters.

Big ideas only make a difference when we act them out. In their book, *Whole Life Worship*, Sam and Sara offer big ideas and biblical foundations that strengthen the connections between the gathered and scattered lives of the people of God – through worship. This pack which accompanies it will help those ideas come to life and find form in your Sunday services and patterns of worship. That's why the pack offers five Sunday service outlines incorporating a wide variety of 'ingredients' in a way that you can take and shape for your context. Sam, Sara and I sit within our own streams of Christian tradition, but we know that God's family is wide and varied.

The outlines are structured thematically. And they align with but don't follow the exact structure of the book. Rather the five themes and the imaginative and practical ideas and resources around each are offered to help different kinds of churches experience gathered worship through the lens of whole-life discipleship. Our worship transforms every area of life: our everyday work and activities, our speech, the way we see things, and, perhaps most importantly, our hearts. And this can happen whoever and wherever we are.

The remainder of the pack is rich and practical. Don't miss its heart. Beyond the pragmatics and the detail lies a heartfelt desire; that the journey you take will lead to your church community, your people discovering the full riches of worship for the whole of their lives.

Neil Hudson

'SO HERE'S WHAT I WANT YOU TO DO, GOD HELPING YOU: TAKE YOUR EVERYDAY, ORDINARY LIFE – YOUR SLEEPING, EATING, GOING-TO-WORK, AND WALKING-AROUND LIFE – AND PLACE IT BEFORE GOD AS AN OFFERING.'

— Romans 12:1 (The Message)

Overview

The *Whole Life Worship Journey Pack* is designed as an accompaniment to the book *Whole Life Worship* (IVP, 2017). The purpose of the *Journey Pack* is to provide a range of activities and practical examples to help your whole church take the next steps on this journey to becoming a whole life worshipping community.

How to use the pack

The pack is organised around five service outlines, providing activities which can be used together as the basis of an entire service. Alternatively, you can pick and choose as you see fit. Those wishing to follow the five service outlines may choose to do so over five consecutive weeks, or perhaps once a month over five months.

For each service we have included a range of possible worship activities. Some relate to the Bible passage for the week. Others explore the service theme more broadly through prayer, praise, song and sending, together with other components of a Sunday service across the traditions. Some suggestions are more formal, some informal. Some will engage all ages, while others are intended for adults. We've signposted some of these characteristics by using a set of icons to guide your choices.

| Informal | Formal | Reflective | All-age friendly |

Those ideas which require some preparation are clearly indicated, but the majority are ready to use. Feel free to adapt them to suit your circumstances: you know best which ideas will work for your congregation in facilitating a meaningful journey of worship.

The USB pen is central to making the most of the pack. More on that overleaf.

What does each service include?

It's helpful to see the shape of the service outlines. Each of the five services is divided into five sections. Within each section is a range of possible activities that you might like to use. You will know best what will work well for your congregation, however we have indicated some of our favourites or ones that we think are central to the theme using this icon: ♡

1. Introduction & Gathering

The first section is an orientation to the theme of the service. It also signposts the key message to look for in the 60–90 second animated videos, which you might want to draw out or reference as the service progresses. We highly recommend that you play these in the service if you can. Following this are some simple ideas, such as prayers and poems, to help people begin to engage in the theme of the service at this point of gathering together.

2. Praise, Prayer & Bible

In this second section there are a variety of activities to pick and choose from – in most cases you will probably want to use just one or two. Praise activities can be easily incorporated into a time of singing. There is a range of creative prayer ideas, some intercessory in nature, others for thanksgiving or confession. Finally, in this section, the Bible ideas offer suggestions for reading the core passage in an interactive or participative manner.

3. Sermon

In the third section we provide framing ideas for a sermon based on the core passage, which we hope will help you in developing a talk suitable to your local church context.

4. Response & Sending

Our fourth section begins with suggestions for ways to help people respond worshipfully to the text. These include reflective moments, as well as more active responses. In session five, the response suggestions incorporate the act of communion. Then there are a variety of prayers, readings and activities to use, as we send one another back into the world to serve the Lord in our everyday contexts.

5. Song Suggestions

Finally, we include a list of suggested songs that fit the theme for the week, which you might choose to incorporate into the service. While we have tried to include a variety of styles, we recognise that everyone has their own approach to music and their own set of regularly used songs or hymns. Nevertheless, we hope some will be familiar to you already, while others you may choose to introduce. Whole life songwriting is a developing area, but there are many existing songs that can work well when framed appropriately. Therefore we have tried to indicate how each song might help draw out the themes explored in the service.

What's on the USB pen?

We recognise that for many churches today, the audio-visual element of Sunday services is key. So, where possible, we have provided materials in a ready-to-use digital format. Where these are available, it is indicated by an icon next to the activity.

 Key to each of the five services is a 1–2 minute animated video which aims to open up the themes of that particular week. As well as being on your USB pen in widely compatible formats, the videos are also available online at licc.org.uk/WholeLifeWorship so you can share them on social media, promote them on your website, or encourage people to watch again and discuss in their small groups.

 Many of the prayers and reflections have ready-to-use PowerPoint slides. Some song lyrics have also been provided on PowerPoint slides where we have the copyright permission to do so. We have included a blank PowerPoint template with graphics that you can use for your own slides too.

 Many churches use their own word projection system, such as SongPro or EasyWorship, so we have provided scripts in unformatted text that can be simply copied and pasted into your preferred software.

Small group study questions

There is a set of small group study questions for each of the five weeks, provided in PDF format. These are designed to help your home groups or other small gatherings talk through the themes of each service. If your church does not fit into the model of having a large Sunday gathering, you could consider using these questions alongside some of the worship resources to create a more discursive experience around the themes. Ready-printed copies are available to buy from licc.org.uk/shop.

Song & hymn lists

Each session includes a short list of recommended songs based on themes for the week. On the USB pen there is a more extensive index of songs and hymns you might like to use, along with links to recordings and sheet music, where available.

'WORSHIP IS ALL-CONSUMING, BECAUSE GOD IS ALL-DESERVING. SO, WE LIVE OUR LIVES EAGER TO BREATHE EVERY BREATH, THINK EVERY THOUGHT, AND DO EVERY DEED FOR THE GLORY OF GOD.'

— Matt Redman

week 1

WORSHIPPING ENGAGES OUR WHOLE LIVES

Key passage: Romans 12:1–2

This session sets the scene for the whole series. It seeks to broaden the congregation's understanding of worship – recognising the importance of church worship, but also giving them a glimpse of how our whole lives can be offered back to God.

We root worship in the gospel, as Paul does in Romans 12. First and foremost, worship is not something we do: it is a response to what God has done in Christ. It is a life lived 'in the light of God's mercy'. In order for this to happen, gathered worship has a role in shaping us, allowing God's perspective to become the reality within which we live out our faith in our everyday lives.

This is an introductory week. The theme of 'shaped by worship' will be unpacked further in Week 2, and the idea of offering our whole selves to God will be picked up again in Week 3. This session is designed to help your congregation begin to think through these issues. So there's no pressure to unpack everything on this Sunday. It won't be the last word on this theme.

Video one: Responding to God in worship in our day to day lives

Gathering

Invitation to Worship

   2 MIN

Today, we come to worship a merciful God,
who offers salvation to all, without prejudice;
everyone who calls on his name will be
saved.

In the light of his wonderful mercy,
in the light of all that he has done for us,
let us bring ourselves to him today.

We bring all that we are,
as an offering of worship,
may it be holy and pleasing to God.

Amen.

Worship on a White Board

  5 MIN

YOU WILL NEED *Whiteboard, pens, a volunteer*

1 Invite people to call out their response to the
   question, "What do you think of when you hear
   the word 'worship'?"
2 Ask your volunteer to write the responses on a
   whiteboard.
3 You should receive quite a variety of responses.
   Note how it can be confusing that so many
   things come under this one umbrella term.
4 Invite people to join you on the journey of
   exploring 'worship' over the course of the series.

Come to Worship

    2 MIN

YOU WILL NEED *Words projected or printed*

This can be used as a call-to-worship prayer, reminding
the congregation that they come bringing their heart,
soul, mind and strength to God.

Leader: Come to worship! Come and give
God all you are!
Put your hearts into it:
make up your minds to give him the best.
All: **With all our hearts we worship.**

Open up your souls and spirits:
let his Spirit move you and touch you.
With all our souls we worship.

Don't switch off your brains:
worship him thoughtfully and intelligently.
With all our minds we worship.

Put your back into it:
never tire of exalting God and showing
others you mean it.
With all our strength we worship.

**All creation praises God,
everything I am comes to bring him the
best I can. Amen.**

© John Leach, used with permission

---

*'TO BRING OUR LIVES AS A DAILY OFFERING, OF WORSHIP TO THE
SERVANT KING.'*

— **Graham Kendrick**, *The Servant King*

Praise, Prayer & Bible

Psalms Praise 5 MIN

YOU WILL NEED *Bibles*

During a time of sung worship …

1 Ask people to open up the book of Psalms at any page.
2 Suggest they look for a line or a verse which strikes them.
3 Invite them to read out the line or verse.

This activity enables the congregation to bring their own contribution during a time of sung worship. It is an easy way to encourage people to participate, as those who might not normally share feel confident reading some words from the Bible. If you feel people might be hesitant, you could prime someone to get the ball rolling. Where possible, it works well to keep a chord or rhythm playing while the verses are read, before launching back into a song.

Reflective Reading of Romans 12:1–2 5 MIN

In this activity, Romans 12:1–2 is read three times, with ample space given for the congregation to reflect on the words. Encourage them to listen to God as you read, and perhaps note down anything which attracts their attention.

1 Firstly, read the passage at a normal, measured pace.
2 The second time, leave a pause at each punctuation mark (as fits the flow of the text).
3 For the final reading, return to the normal pace, emphasising the text in bold.

> Therefore, I urge you, brothers and sisters, **in view of God's mercy**, to offer your bodies as a **living sacrifice, holy and pleasing** to God—**this is your true and proper worship. Do not conform** to the pattern of this world, **but be transformed** by the renewing of your mind. Then you will be able to test and approve what God's will is—his good, pleasing and perfect will.
>
> — **Romans 12:1–2** (NIV)

'CHRIST BE IN MY SPEAKING, EVERY WORD A BLESSING, PURE AND NOT DECEIVING, GRACE TO ALL WHO HEAR'

— **Stuart Townend & Simon Brading,** *Christ be in my Waking*

KEY 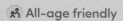 Informal • Formal • Reflective • All-age friendly • Favouri

Psalm 67 Prayer Flow ⬛ ⬛ ⬛ ⬛ 10 MIN

YOU WILL NEED *Words projected or printed*

This flow of worship reminds us of God's intense interest in the whole world. It uses one verse from Psalm 67 as a repeated refrain. You might like to use the first line of the hymn 'Holy, holy, holy' as printed below, or use your own tune.

SING May the peoples praise you, God; may all the peoples praise you.

SAY May God be gracious to us and bless us and make his face shine on us.

PAUSE FOR SILENT OR OPEN PRAYERS FOR NEEDS IN YOUR CHURCH COMMUNITY

SING May the peoples praise you, God; may all the peoples praise you.

SAY So that your ways may be known on earth, your salvation among all nations.

PAUSE FOR SILENT OR OPEN PRAYERS FOR NEEDS ACROSS THE WORLD

SING May the peoples praise you, God; may all the peoples praise you.

SAY May the nations be glad and sing for joy, for you rule the peoples with equity and guide the nations of the earth.

PAUSE FOR SILENT OR OPEN PRAYERS FOR GOVERNMENTS, ELECTIONS AND LEADERS

SING May the peoples praise you, God; may all the peoples praise you.

SAY The land yields its harvest; God, our God, blesses us.

PAUSE FOR SILENT OR OPEN PRAYERS OF THANKS FOR GOD'S PROVISION

SAY May God bless us still, so that all the ends of the earth will fear him.

SING May the peoples praise you, God; may all the peoples praise you.

May the peo-ples praise you, God; may all the peo-ples praise you.

Sermon

Core Message: Our offering of worship to God can look remarkably ordinary.

Key passage: Romans 12:1–2

Sometimes Paul doesn't say what we might have expected. In fact, sometimes he says the totally unexpected. For 11 chapters of the book of Romans he has explored all that God has done to rescue a world that rebelled against his designs and desires. He knows that this is the good news; the gospel. And that once we embrace the gospel, we will want to worship. So far, so expected.

But for a group of people who think they know what worship looks like, Paul's words are surprising. The Jews in the church in Rome had their own history of worshipping: with temples, offerings, sacrifices. Gentiles had their own temples, their own offerings, their own sacrifices. And Paul's message to both groups is that worship is so much more: it involves our living bodies.

That's the bit that would have shocked. Living bodies are not that perfect. They tend to be misshapen, badly used, worn out. They are, not to put too fine a point on it, too ordinary. But that's what Paul thinks worship is all about. So what is worship?

1 **It's a response to God's mercy.**
   Paul has spent 11 chapters exploring what God's mercy has done for us. Once you see that God is the source of all life and that he has done so much to bring salvation to everyone, there is so much to give thanks for. In fact, Paul has said that one of the marks of a pagan world is that they do not give thanks to God for all they have (Romans 1:21). Our worship focuses our thankful hearts.

2 **It involves our** *'everyday, ordinary life – our sleeping, eating, going-to-work, and walking-around life'* **– Romans 12:1, (The Message).**
   Worship is not just an inward, private, 'spiritual' activity, it involves every ordinary aspect of our lives. So it has to be seen as more than an hour on Sunday. Our worship should have no sacred-secular divide. We are called to worship God in our homes, on our streets, in our workplaces. We can worship through our attitudes, our finances, our politics, our leisure. All these things and more can be done in God's presence, in God's ways and for God's glory.

3 **It is a decision to be shaped in a particular way.**
   Paul links our worship with changing the way we think. He knows that Rome has a certain way of doing things. But he knows that a follower of Jesus will no longer necessarily conform to Rome's ways because he sees them through God's eyes. And as that change in perspective shapes and changes us, as we see the world differently, we discover ever more deeply what God's will is for our lives – in the ordinary places in which we find ourselves.

So this one hour on Sunday is the tip of an iceberg that is made up of 168 hours per week. Our worship involves our whole lives, because it all matters.

We will be going deeper into these themes over the series. For now, though, consider how this passage challenges assumptions about worship, and what God might be calling his people to do in response.

Response & Sending

Reflective Prayer ⬛ ▣ ◷ 5 MIN

As you lead this prayer, allow time for the congregation to consider their personal response by pausing between each paragraph.

Leader: Father God, we reflect on your mercy. We consider the forgiveness you have granted us through your Son, Jesus Christ. We know we were bought at a price. In view of God's mercy, we offer our bodies as a living sacrifice, holy and pleasing to God.
All: **This is our true and proper worship.**

We pray for the grace and strength to offer our all: the tasks we complete, the relationships we value, the activities we enjoy, and the possessions we own. Help us to glorify you with all these things. In view of God's mercy, we offer our bodies as a living sacrifice, holy and pleasing to God.
This is our true and proper worship.

We pray that you would renew our minds by the power of the Holy Spirit. Help us to be wary of conforming to the patterns of this world, make us watchful to see what is shaping our view of the world. In view of God's mercy, we offer our bodies as a living sacrifice, holy and pleasing to God.
This is our true and proper worship.

Finally, we pray for help to know your will. Give us a discerning spirit to know – whether at home, at work or wherever we are – what your good, pleasing and perfect will might be. In view of God's mercy, we offer our bodies as a living sacrifice, holy and pleasing to God.
This is our true and proper worship.

We pray all of these things in the name of Christ,

Amen

Gift Box Worship ⚇ ◷ 10 MIN

YOU WILL NEED *Box, wrapping paper, decorations, Post-it notes, pens*

This activity allows people to consider what aspect of their life they might like to offer to God as worship this week.

1 Wrap a shoe box, or another box with a lid, in gift-wrap paper, adding bows and ribbons to make it look special. Put it in a prominent place.
2 Give everyone a post-it note and a pen.
3 Invite them to think about what aspect of their life this week they want to offer back to God as worship.
4 Ask them to draw that aspect on their post-it, and come and put it in the gift box as a sign of commitment.

You might want to use a song that fits the theme as people are bringing their papers to put in the box. Hold the box to say a prayer of dedication at the end of the time.

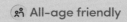

Responsive Reading ♡ ⋮⋮ ♙ 📖 ⏱ 5 MIN

YOU WILL NEED *Words projected or printed*

Invite the congregation to join in a response to the paraphrased text below from Romans 12. They respond each time to the phrase 'Just do it' with the line 'This is our worship.' Depending on your context, you may prefer to substitute 'Let's do it' for 'Just do it', but either way try to ensure the tone is encouraging.

Leader: In Christ we, though many, form one body, and each member belongs to all the others. We all have different gifts.

If it's prophesying – Just do it: All: **This is our worship.**
If it's serving – Just do it: **This is our worship.**
If it's teaching – Just do it: **This is our worship.**
If it's encouraging – Just do it: **This is our worship.**
If it's giving – Just do it: **This is our worship.**
If it's leading – Just do it: **This is our worship.**
If it's showing mercy – Just do it: **This is our worship.**

Love must be sincere. Hate what's evil; cling to what's good.
Be joyful in hope, patient in trouble, faithful in prayer.
Be generous and invite people around.
Just do it: **This is our worship.**

Don't hit back, but show love. Care for each other, be a friend to those who are alone.
Don't take revenge, if a bully is hungry and thirsty, give him food and drink.
Just do it: **This is our worship.**

The idea can be developed one stage further by then asking the congregation to say what they will be doing in the week – the ordinary things they'll do on Monday morning at work, home or wherever they find themselves. When someone shares something, (for example, 'teaching a class', 'washing the car', 'making a spreadsheet') you can respond 'Just do it' and the congregation can encourage them, 'This is our worship.'

'WERE THE WHOLE REALM OF NATURE MINE, THAT WERE AN OFFERING FAR TOO SMALL. LOVE SO AMAZING, SO DIVINE, DEMANDS MY SOUL, MY LIFE, MY ALL.'

— **Isaac Watts,** *When I Survey the Wondrous Cross*

Song Suggestions

Gathering

As we gather (Whatever we do) **by Joel Payne** — *modern song*
All of life is worship

To God be the glory **by Fanny Crosby** — *traditional hymn*
Coming through Christ that the whole earth might hear

Praise

Praise to the Lord, the Almighty 🖥 **by Joachim Neander, Catherine Winkworth and others (Jubilate words)** — *traditional hymn, modernised words*
God is King and Lord of all creation

Unbroken praise **by Matt Redman, Jonas Myrin** — *modern song*
Praise continues into all of our lives

In the light of your mercy 🖥 **by Sam Hargreaves** — *modern song*
Romans 12:1 – offering our whole life to God

Response

Christ be in my waking 💟 **by Stuart Townend, Simon Brading** — *modern hymn*
Whole of life is for Jesus

God in my living (Everything) 💟 **by Tim Hughes** — *modern song*
God is involved in all of life

In my life Lord **by Bob Kilpatrick** — *modern song*
Giving all to Christ, can be adapted – 'in my work/home/school'

Sending

I will worship (You're worthy of my praise) **by David Ruis** — *modern song*
Heart, soul, mind and strength – giving all to God

Forth in thy name *or* Forth in your name (Be glorified) **by Graham Kendrick, based on Charles Wesley** — *traditional hymn, modernised style*
Declaration of us being sent out to worship

Called by Christ to be disciples **by Martin E. Leckebusch** — *traditional hymn*
Emphasising discipleship and the serving of God's Kingdom
purposes in our everyday work and roles

 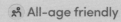

Notes

week 2

WORSHIPPING OFFERS US FRESH INSIGHT

Key passage: Ephesians 1:15–23

In order to live whole lives of worship, we need to see the world differently. There are many competing 'stories' which act as lenses through which we can see the world. For example, the 'success' story which encourages us to believe that life is about getting a good job, a good house and having great holidays. They may be blessings, but is that what life is really about? Others may be driven by a 'fear' story, which portrays everyone as a potential enemy, likely to take advantage. So life is a drive to stay safe. Safety may be sensible, and important in certain contexts. But is life all about staying safe?

The lenses through which we see our lives will shape how we live them. God's story helps us to see life from his perspective, putting his purposes at the centre.

So gathered worship is an opportunity to keep revisiting that big story of creation, fall, redemption and re-creation. It's a time when you can lead people into a deeper understanding of God's heart and mission and the implications of this for us today as we find our place in his story. This week is designed to give your congregation a new perspective on their lives and frontlines as places where God is working through them to bring about his purposes. And gathered worship is also a time when we're reminded of God's power to do just that.

We've included ideas for intercession, because praying for the world can be part of seeing the world differently. Also included are creative resources for engaging with creeds, which are ways of telling God's bigger story.

> Video two: Come, worship, see. This is a vital invitation to any church community.

KEY ⊶ Informal   ⊞ Formal   ☁ Reflective   ⚲ All-age friendly   ♡ Favourite

Gathering

Invitation to Worship
   1 MIN

We have come to worship a powerful God.
The God who raised Christ from the dead,
who seated him at his right hand in the
heavenly realms, far above all rule and
authority, power and dominion,
and every other name, now or in the future.

May the eyes of our hearts be opened today,
with wisdom and revelation from the Holy
Spirit,
to know, really know, the hope to which he
has called us,
and the glorious plans he has for all
creation.

We have come to worship a powerful God,
let us turn to him in awe and adoration.

Amen.

Looking through Lenses
   5–10 MIN

YOU WILL NEED *Copies of cardboard glasses printed on A3 card (on USB), pens, scissors*

1 Distribute printed copies of the glasses template.
2 Invite people to cut out their glasses. (You might like to pre-cut these if you are able.)
3 Ask people to talk together about the different 'lenses' they use to see the world – through social media, newspapers, TV, politics, celebrities, at work, when they are with different people.
4 Invite them to write or draw the different perspectives on the frames.

Thank you to Guy Houchen for the 3D glasses template

Open Us Up   1 MIN

YOU WILL NEED *Words projected or printed*

This could be used as a gathering prayer, or somewhere close to the start of the service. It can flow into singing the song 'Open the eyes of my heart'.

All: **Open us up, God**
Leader: for all you have for us today.

Open our eyes, God
to see you reflected in every human face.

Open our hearts, God
to feel your compassion for this broken world.

Open our ears, God
to hear the whisper of your Spirit and the wisdom of your word.

Open our hands, God
this is your ministry, your Kingdom, your power, your glory.

Open our lips, God
that our mouths may sing out your praise.

Lenses Reflection
 3 MIN

YOU WILL NEED *PowerPoint projected, appropriate background music*

Invite the congregation to think about the different 'lenses' they see the world through while watching the photo montage PowerPoint. It's helpful to choose some instrumental background music to play, or you can ask your musicians to play live underneath the presentation.

Praise, Prayer & Bible

Jesus is Lord 👥 📖 🕐 2 MIN

The following prayer is based on Philippians 2 using the phrase 'Jesus is Lord', which can work as a lens, allowing us to see the world differently. If Jesus is Lord over the whole earth, that changes how we view our work, our homes, our frontlines and so on. You could try varying the volume using your hand: when it is raised high people should respond loudly, and when it is low they should respond quietly. Begin with your hand high and move it down through the first section, before building the response through the second section.

After saying the prayer, you might like to invite people to think about one situation in their lives or the world where it's harder to believe that 'Jesus is Lord'. Get them to summarise the situation in three to four words: 'in my workplace', 'over my finances', 'in the pub', 'in the toddler group' etc. Finally, invite people to speak out those situations one by one, as the congregation responds 'Jesus is Lord'.

Leader: Equal with God:
All: **Jesus is Lord.**
Emptied himself: **Jesus is Lord.**
Came as a slave: **Jesus is Lord.**
Found as a man: **Jesus is Lord.**
Humbly obeyed: **Jesus is Lord.**
Went to his death: **Jesus is Lord.**
Death on a cross: **Jesus is Lord.**

GETTING GRADUALLY LOUDER

God raised him up: **Jesus is Lord.**
Gave him the name: **Jesus is Lord.**
Higher than all: **Jesus is Lord.**
Every knee bow: **Jesus is Lord.**
All tongues confess: **Jesus is Lord!**
Glory to God! **Jesus is Lord!**

© **Michael Perry, used with permission**

Collage Prayers 👥 🕐 5 MIN

YOU WILL NEED *Newspapers from the previous week, glue sticks, A3 paper, felt-tip pens*

The idea for this activity is that people fill an A3 sheet with items from the newspaper which they wish to pray for. If children are involved in the activity, you may need to be mindful of inappropriate or frightening pictures in some newspapers and, depending on their age, the felt-tip pens!

1 Invite the congregation to form groups of four to six people.
2 Give each group a newspaper, glue, a pen and a sheet of paper.
3 Take a moment to pray, asking God to open people's eyes to the problems and suffering in the world.
4 Ask the groups to flick through the newspapers and tear out any pictures or headlines that they wish to pray for.

5 In the final few minutes, ask the groups to form a one-line prayer and write it over their newspaper cut-outs with the felt-tip pen.
6 If you have time, ask the groups to take turns saying their one-line prayer. You could invite the rest of the congregation to respond in some way, for example by saying: *'Thank you God, that you see the world, and you hear our prayer. Amen.'*

Vision of Hope Prayer ♡ ⁘ 🗐 ⏱ 10–15 MIN

These intercessory prayers are based on the passage for this week. They encourage the congregation to pray for the world and the people around them, and to see them through God's eyes. Allow time for the congregation to consider their personal response by pausing between each paragraph.

Leader: Paul wrote to the Ephesians that he had not stopped giving thanks for them, and kept remembering them in his prayers. Who do you need to give thanks to God for today? Who needs to be remembered in your prayers? Bring that person before God in the silence.

Open the eyes of our hearts, Lord.
All: **Give us a vision of your hope.**
Paul prayed that they might know the God and Father of our Lord Jesus Christ, through the Holy Spirit. Who do you know who needs to know God for the first time, or who needs to know God better? Pray for that person in the silence.

Open the eyes of our hearts, Lord.
Give us a vision of your hope.
Paul asked that they might know God's power which raised Christ from the dead and seated him over every authority, ruler and title. When you look at the world, do you see rulers and authorities using their power for good or for evil? Pray for powerful leaders, and ask God to help you trust him that he is the ultimate authority.

Open the eyes of our hearts, Lord.
Give us a vision of your hope.
Paul reminded them that Jesus is the head of the church and that all things are under his rule. In your everyday life and on your frontline, what issues do you need to entrust to Jesus? In the silence, ask him to be Lord of your situations and struggles.

'And may the eyes of our hearts be enlightened to know the hope to which he has called us, the riches of his glorious inheritance, and the incomparably great power for us who believe.' (Ephesians 1:18)
Open the eyes of our hearts, Lord.
Give us a vision of your hope.

Amen.

Creeds

Introduction to the Nicene Creed

YOU WILL NEED *Words projected or printed*

Whether or not you say a creed, such as the Nicene Creed, on a regular basis, we can easily miss out on the life-changing implications of these words. It can therefore be helpful to introduce the Nicene Creed by reminding the congregation of its significance. When we recite the creed we retell a radically different understanding of how the world was formed, what sustains it and where it is ultimately headed. This is in contrast to the stories told to us by the media, politics, advertisers and academics. We are rooting ourselves in a counter-cultural story, and this perspective can and should dramatically change how we live our lives in the world. So encourage your congregation to say it with the 'eyes of their hearts' open to this transforming narrative.

Credal Prayer

YOU WILL NEED *Words projected or printed*

This prayer reminds us of God's big story, specifically relating it to our everyday lives.

All: **We believe in God the creator,**
Leader: who spoke everything into being by his Word and his Spirit,
the physical and the spiritual, the extraordinary and the everyday.
Open our eyes, God, to see your big story.

We believe in God the just,
who sees our mistakes and our fallenness,
who judges sin and will right every wrong.
Open our eyes, God, to see your big story.

We believe in God the incarnate,
who came as one of us in Jesus Christ,
who knows our weakness and yet chose obedience.
Open our eyes, God, to see your big story.

We believe in God the saviour,
who reconciled all things to himself on the cross,
and commits us to the message of reconciliation.
Open our eyes, God, to see your big story.

We believe in God the restorer,
who will come again to renew creation,
and calls us to play our part as we long for that completeness.
Open our eyes, God, to live your big story.

Amen.

 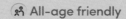

All-Age Creed 🧑‍🤝‍🧑 📖 🕐 1 MIN

This idea uses hand actions to remember God's big story.

> In the big story *DRAW AN ARCH WITH YOUR RIGHT INDEX FINGER ACROSS ALL THE FINGERS OF YOUR LEFT HAND, AND REPEAT THIS FOR EACH REPETITION OF THIS LINE*
> God made it all. *HOLD YOUR LEFT THUMB*
> In the big story
> we had a big fall. *HOLD YOUR LEFT INDEX FINGER*
>
> In the big story
> Jesus moved in. *HOLD YOUR LEFT MIDDLE FINGER*
> In the big story
> he died for our sin. *HOLD YOUR LEFT RING FINGER*
>
> In the big story
> God will make all things new. *HOLD YOUR LEFT LITTLE FINGER*
> This is God's story
> it's your story too. *POINT OUTWARDS WITH BOTH INDEX FINGERS*

Creed Song Suggestions

You might choose to incorporate the following songs into this part of the service:

Our Father everlasting (This I believe, The Creed) by Ben Fielding, Matt Crocker – *modern song*
Modern setting of the Apostles' Creed

We believe in God the Father (Because we believe) by Jamie Harvill, Nancy Gordon – *modern song*
Creed in call-response format

Jesus is Lord, the cry that echoes by Stuart Townend, Keith Getty – *modern hymn*
Picking up on the bigger story of what God is doing in the world

'WORSHIP IS A SUBJECT THAT SHOULD DOMINATE OUR LIVES SEVEN DAYS A WEEK.'

— David Peterson, *Engaging with God*

Sermon

Core Message: Worship shows us the bigger picture of what God is doing in and through us in the world.

Key passage: Ephesians 1:15–23

If you wanted the apostle Paul to pray for your church today, what would you want him to pray? Our prayers tell us what is most important to us. Tell me your prayers, and I'll tell you what really matters to you. The letter to the church in Ephesus was most likely designed to be read in many different churches, so we might be able to see what Paul thinks 'ordinary' churches need. What we discover is that Paul believed that they/we need to see better. He prays for a whole life vision: a vision that sees Jesus filling everything in every way. No area of life was to be untouched.

Ephesians 1:3–14 is one long cascade of praise. Paul wants the Ephesians to be captivated not by all the temples of Diana or the symbols of the Roman Empire, but by a sense of what God has done. He knows that this is what will help these early Christians to stand firm and act courageously. And in the midst of this brilliant passage, he prays for the churches. And that prayer is still so relevant for us today.

He prays that we might have

1 **A compelling vision**

   Paul uses a wide range of words and metaphors to paint a vivid picture of how our salvation is linked to God's widest purposes, for the whole of his creation (v 10). He wants us to see just how comprehensive our salvation is.

2 **A renewing vision**

   He prays that we will know God better (v 17), that we will appreciate the God who has called us to live for him. Alongside this prayer is one that we might grasp a vision of our future (the hope of v 18), of who is with us (the saints in v 18), and of the power that is within us (the same power that raised Jesus from the dead, vs 19–20). If God answered that fantastic prayer, how would it change our everyday lives?

3 **A whole life vision**

   Ephesus had its own story of how the world worked, but the Christians embraced a whole life vision. It was the vision of Jesus ruling over all ('the fullness of him who fills everything in every way' vs 22–23). No area of life can be left untouched once we see this vision of Jesus ruling over all.

When we worship together we help one another see things differently. Prayers, songs, creeds, readings, testimonies and more remind us of God's bigger story, and give us the opportunity to be refreshed with God's resurrection power. This empowers and inspires us to live this vision of life out on our frontlines, glorifying God in everything we do.

The goal of this prayer would be greater confidence for the minority of Ephesian citizens who worshipped Jesus. What could it mean for us?

Response & Sending

Looking through Lenses 👥 📖 🕐 10 MIN

YOU WILL NEED *Copies of the cardboard glasses, pens, coloured cellophane, sticky tape*

This activity uses the cardboard glasses that were made in the earlier gathering idea.

Give out coloured cellophane, and invite people to think about one issue in their life they need to see through God's eyes. It could be a situation at work, home or elsewhere that they are struggling with. What would it mean to see it from God's perspective? How can they worship God in the midst of that situation? Invite them to stick the cellophane into the eyeholes of their glasses, committing themselves to seeing with God's eyes this week.

Prayer Ministry 💠 ☁ 🕐 10 MIN

Create space for people to receive a fresh touch of God's Holy Spirit, in order that they might see the world through God's eyes. You could do this by leading quiet songs, or leaving silence, or creating a prayer ministry space where people can go and be prayed for.

'BIBLICAL WORSHIP IS A RESPONSE TO GOD'S REVELATION OF HIMSELF, EMPOWERED BY THE HOLY SPIRIT, WHICH FINDS EXPRESSION IN EVERY ASPECT OF HUMAN LIFE AND EXPERIENCE.'

— **John Risbridger,** *The Message of Worship*

Go into the Whole World 👥 🕐 5 MIN

Jesus told his disciples

> ' ... you will receive power when the Holy Spirit comes on you; and you will
> be my witnesses in Jerusalem, and in all Judea and Samaria, and to the
> ends of the earth.'
>
> — Acts 1:8

1 Ask the congregation to share in groups one place that they will visit in the coming week, perhaps another city, or something more local, like the bowling club or the toddler group.

2 Explain that, just before his ascension in Acts 1, Jesus sent his disciples out into the whole world. We are his disciples today and the places people have mentioned are included in Jesus' sending. We need to ask Jesus to help us see the places we are going to through his eyes – as places he loves and wants us to be witnesses in.

3 Ask people in their groups to send one another out by customising the words above to their particular situation. For example, 'You received power when the Holy Spirit came on you, and you will be his witness in the toddler group, and to the ends of the earth.'

'CHRIST HAS NO BODY ON EARTH NOW BUT YOURS, NO HANDS
BUT YOURS, NO FEET BUT YOURS. YOURS ARE THE EYES THROUGH
WHICH HE LOOKS COMPASSION ON THIS WORLD. YOURS ARE THE
FEET WITH WHICH HE WALKS TO DO GOOD. YOURS ARE THE HANDS
WITH WHICH HE BLESSES ALL THE WORLD.'

— **Teresa of Avila**

Song Suggestions

Gathering

Open the eyes of my heart by **Paul Baloche** – *modern song*
Simple song, opening our hearts to God's greatness

Behold us, Lord, a little space by **John Ellerton** – *traditional hymn*
Meeting God in church, work and home

Be the God of all my Sundays by **Martin E. Leckebusch** – *traditional hymn*
Serving God through our everyday lifestyle

Praise & Prayer

Christ was raised ♡ ▣ by **Sam Hargreaves** – *modern hymn*
The impact of the resurrection on the whole of life and creation

He's my Saviour by **Joel Payne** – *short refrain*
Focus on Jesus. Alternative lines can be improvised

Lord you hear the cry (Lord have mercy) ♡ ▣ by **Geraldine Latty** – *modern song*
God's heart for the world, intercessory song

O Lord hear my prayer by **Jacques Berthier (Taizé)** – *chant style*
Intercessory song, simple and repeated

Response

I will sing the wondrous story by **Francis H. Rowley** – *traditional hymn*
Reminder to focus on the story of Christ

On that day by **Geraldine Latty** – *gospel feel*
Looking forward to the end of the story, and the impact that has on now

When I hear the stories (The way that you see) by **Steve Squires** – *all-age song*
Asking God that we would see the world through his eyes

Sending

Be thou my vision by **Eleanor Henrietta Hull, Mary Elizabeth Byrne** – *traditional hymn*
Celtic hymn, asking God to help us see the world through his eyes

We seek your Kingdom by **N. Robinson, A. Flannagan, G. Hunter** – *modernised hymn*
Mentions a range of ways we can serve in public life. To the tune of 'Abide with me'

Come set your rule and reign by **Rend Collective** – *modern song*
Calling out to God to transform the world and our local area through us

Notes

week 3

WORSHIPPING TRANSFORMS OUR ORDINARY ACTIONS

Key passage: Colossians 3:12–17

In this week we go deeper with a point we introduced in Week 1 – that everything we do can be offered as worship. Our worship flows out of the understanding of our core identity as God's holy people, chosen and dearly loved. As we gather together we experience a deeper reality of dwelling in Christ – through all that we do and think and sing and say in that time. It can be transformative. But that deep delight in our identity means that our expressions of worship cannot just be about our experiences in church: our worship must spill out into 'whatever we do'.

This is a week that can address the temptation to live a sacred-secular divided life, where we think the really important aspects of life are those that are connected to our church life, or our spiritual life, rather than our ordinary lives and the places where we have to roll our sleeves up and get stuck into the tasks that we have to complete each day.

To help your congregation engage with this we have included prayers which focus on the 'works of our hands'. There are also confession ideas which cover those times when we have not used our hands to glorify God. A good number of the ideas this week are tactile and physical, emphasising the earthed nature of worship which should not be merely 'spiritual' or invisible, but grounded in solid reality.

> Video three: Inviting God into our everyday work, tasks and chores – how liberating

Gathering

In the Beginnning

 2 MIN

YOU WILL NEED *Words projected or printed*

This locates our gathering to worship in the wider story of God's creation and continuing involvement in the world. If you use the PowerPoint this adds an engaging visual dimension. It works well to play instrumental music underneath the words (e.g. *Takk* on the Sigur Ros album by the same name), but music is not essential.

Leader: In the beginning, God created the heavens and the earth.
In the empty void and crushing darkness, God spoke light into being.
All: **Creator God, bring light into our darkness.**

In the beginning, God took eternity and formed time and space,
seasons, days and years.
Creator God, fill and shape the time you have given us.

In the beginning, God took land and sea and filled them with life of every kind.
Creator God, help us find our place within your diverse creation.

In the beginning, God spoke his very image, and in the returning echo formed humanity.
Creator God, open our eyes to see you reflected in every human face.

In the beginning, God created,
and it was good.

© Mark Earey, used with permission

Question/Play-dough Activity   5–10 MIN

YOU WILL NEED *Bought or home-made play-dough*

Get people to share one task they have done with their hands this week then make a model of it out of play-dough. Once made, the models could be placed on a central table, visible through the service. You might ask people to quietly consider with what attitude they approached that task.

Bringing an Item 10 MIN

YOU WILL NEED *To ask people to bring an item that represents their daily life*

Ask the congregation to bring in an item from their everyday life to church on this particular Sunday. It should be something that they use on a daily basis, preferably something that symbolises their frontline. For a student it might be a book, for many people with desk-jobs it might be a laptop, for some it might be their knitting, their cooking utensils or any other tools. Provide post-it notes for those who have not brought an item and invite them to draw a picture of it. Ask the congregation to get into groups, to 'show-and-tell' their item. If your congregation numbers fewer than 20, it might be possible for each person to share with the whole group.

These can be used in the response (see later).

Praise & Prayer

Junk Percussion 🖥 🕐 10 MIN

YOU WILL NEED *Small hand-drums or junk percussion*

To introduce the idea of worshipping with your actions, you could do some clapping or play percussion instruments. Sometimes we can over-spiritualise worship, keeping it in our words, minds and hearts. This activity can remind us of Jesus' instruction to love the Lord with all our 'strength', our physical beings. It also includes people in musical worship who may not find singing so easy. And it can be fun!

This can be done as a game, where the leader claps a four-beat rhythm and everyone claps or hits the rhythm back. Then transition into your sung worship time, by teaching a rhythm along to a worship song, or asking people to play to the rhythm of a worship phrase ('Praise the Lord', 'Glory to God', etc). Give space for the instruments to have a 'solo' moment, and emphasise that hitting a drum can be just as much an act of worship as singing or playing. There are more tips on this theme at engageworship.org

Local Area Images 🔘 🕐 5 MIN

YOU WILL NEED *Someone with one to two hours to prepare a PowerPoint or video*

Create a montage of images of your local area. These can be sourced from church members sending in pictures of their 'frontlines': their homes, streets, workplaces and leisure spots. You could put these in a video or PowerPoint presentation and overlay the question, 'How do we worship here?'

You could also use these as background images when singing one of your usual praise songs or hymns, reminding the congregation that their praise extends out into their weekly life.

Scribble Page 🔘 📱 🕐 10 MIN

YOU WILL NEED *Print-outs of the sheet, pens, quiet background music*

Distribute a print-out of Colossians 3:12–17 to each person. Explain that this is a simple opportunity for each person to reflect on the Bible reading. If they find it helpful they can write or doodle on the sheets, but they may prefer just to read the text and turn it over in their mind.

Works of Our Hands ♥ ⦿ ▤ ◔ 3 MIN

This is a formal, led time of intercession, focusing on the works of our hands bringing glory to God.

Father, we pray for our world, and for the works of our hands every day.

We think of those who use their hands for care. The nurses, doctors, carers, mothers, fathers and countless other people who help and heal. God, strengthen these hands when they are weak. May their gentle touch be an act of worship to you.

We think of those who use their hands with technology and science. For the programmers, technicians, engineers, labourers and everyone else who builds and develops. God, thank you for innovation. May it be used for the good of your whole creation, and to glorify you.

We think of those who use their hands for art. For the writers, musicians, filmmakers, florists and everyone else who beautifies and reveals truth. God, may our creative fingers reveal more of who you are and speak prophetically into your world.

We think of those who use their hands with money and governance. For the bankers, politicians, businesspeople, managers and everyone who organises and allocates resources. God, help those hands to act fairly, honestly and bravely in a world which wants them to be selfish and timid.

We think of those who use their hands for hard physical work. For the cleaners, lifters, packers, sorters and everyone else whose strength and commitment brings order to your world. God, make us grateful for those who toil. Show them that their vital work brings praise to you.

We think of those who wish they could use their hands more than they do. For the unemployed, the depressed, the physically limited and everyone else who struggles to lift their hands. May they find comfort in your love, and may we value their unique contribution to your Kingdom.

May the works of our hands glorify you, as we are held in your hands.

Amen.

Prayer (continued)

Hand Prayer 🔵 🔵 🔵 10 MIN

YOU WILL NEED *Quiet background music*

Ask the congregation to find a comfortable position, and lead them in the following prayerful reflection time. Try to speak slowly, leaving plenty of pauses for personal reflection. You might like to play some quiet music in the background.

I want to invite you to spend a moment looking at your hands. Turn them over and look at them from every angle. What do you notice? Are your hands small or large, smooth or rough, warm or cold? Do you see scars? What do they remind you of? Perhaps you are wearing jewellery? Are there memories attached to any bracelets or rings? Now, think through an ordinary day, and note all the things you do with your hands. From turning off the alarm clock in the morning, to switching the bedside lamp at night, draw to mind all the things that you use your hands for. Spend a moment thanking God for the good things that you have remembered: material provision, family members, fulfilling work and spare time activities.

Now, I invite you to close your hands into fists. We read in Colossians 3 that whatever we do, whether in word or deed, we are to do in Jesus' name, giving thanks to the Father. Let us spend a moment considering how we use our hands in ways which are not glorifying to God. Perhaps these are things that weigh us down with guilt and regret: words typed, grasping for what is not ours or indulging our own desires. Or perhaps, ours is more a sin of omission, of holding our hands tightly shut, when we should be generous with love or possessions. Our God of mercy invites you to bring these things before him in confession.

I invite you to open your fists now, and turn your hands with your palms up, as if receiving a gift. By Christ's death on the cross, God forgives your sin when you confess it to him. Receive his forgiveness and freedom from guilt. With your hands still open, what might you be able to offer back? Are there things in your daily life that can be done more purposefully for God? Can you imagine your daily tasks as being offered as worship to him?

Let's pray: Father you created us to do good and to bring glory to you. Now, take all that we are, our words, our deeds and the work of our hands, and use them as we live as people of your Kingdom, and for your praise and honour.
In the name of Christ,

Amen.

KEY   Informal   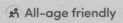 Formal   🔵 Reflective   👥 All-age friendly   Favour

Sermon

Core Message: Worship is not just our songs and prayers, but also our actions and attitudes in the world.

Key passage: Colossians 3:12–17

What does it mean to be an everyday worshipper? How do you really worship in work, school etc? Does it involve singing quietly under your breath as you wait at the checkout? Whistling 'Shine, Jesus, Shine' as you dust the dining room? Offering prayer at the beginning of business meetings?

Not necessarily!

It means that whatever we do, we do for the glory of God. Our whole lives become our offering of worship.

When Paul writes to the Colossians and urges them to do everything in the name of the Lord Jesus, while overflowing with gratitude, this is not something else on their 'to-do' list. It is to flow out of a new identity, to be fuelled by a new motivation, and to be worked out in their everyday circumstance.

1 **Our Identity: Who We Are**

   We are people who have 'taken off the old self' (v 9) and put on a new identity (v 10) – one that increases our understanding of what it means to be created in God's image. This new identity also means that we learn to act differently towards one another (vs 11–14).

2 **Our Motivation: Why We Can**

   Paul urges the Christians to allow the peace of Christ and the Word of Christ to work out in our lives together (vs 15–16). This happens as we teach one another and as we sing together. Our worship together is the overflow of our new life in Christ. We learn a new story of the world and our place in it, we hear a new word spoken to us, and in songs and psalms we sing this new story to one another.

3 **Our Situations: Wherever We Are**

   Everything is changed: whatever we do – at work, in school, at home, in the local shop – we can now do in the name of Jesus and to the glory of God the Father. Worship is whole life and it is worked out in the very practical ways we relate to other people, do our work, spend our money and so on.

'WORSHIP IS WHERE ABOVE ALL WE PROCLAIM OUR PRIORITIES, AND ARE FORMED BY THE SPIRIT THROUGH WHAT WE PROCLAIM, AND PERHAPS ESPECIALLY BY WHAT WE SING.'

— **Graham Cray,** *In Spirit and Truth*

Response & Sending

Commissioning for All 🎛 📄 ⏱ 5–10 MIN

It is quite common to pray commissioning prayers for missionaries, ordained ministers or roles within church life. However, every member of the church has a place to which they are called by God – their 'frontline'. This activity reminds us that the whole church body is called, gifted and sent to serve Christ in the world. This is ultimately an act of worship – bringing glory to God through our daily service, relationships and attitudes.

The following prayer can be said over the whole congregation. It could be useful to give people a moment's quiet first to consider the 'frontline' to which they are being commissioned. Then invite people to stand and respond to each question with, "By the grace of God, we will."

Leader: Will you pray that you will experience God's presence on your frontline?
All: **By the grace of God, we will.**

Will you search for his will and let it be done in your day-to-day decisions and deeds?
By the grace of God, we will.

Will you reflect what it means to be a follower of Jesus in all your relationships?
By the grace of God, we will.

Will you live in such a way that others will want to know what Christ means to you?
By the grace of God, we will.

Will you make a conscious effort to minister and witness across all types of barriers in a sympathetic, loving and patient manner?
By the grace of God, we will.

When conditions allow, will you invite others to acknowledge Christ as Lord?
By the grace of God, we will.

We commend one another to this work and pledge our prayers, encouragement and support. May the Holy Spirit guide and strengthen us, that in this and in all things we may do God's will to the service of Jesus Christ.

Question/Play-dough Idea 👥 ⏱ 5–10 MIN

YOU WILL NEED *Play-dough models created earlier (see page 31)*

Come back to the play-dough models people made at the beginning of the service. Invite them to think about the physical tasks they will do in the coming week. What difference would it make if they did those for God?

Invite them to re-form the play-dough into a new model, which represents how they want to worship God with their hands this week. Alternatively, invite people to share this with a neighbour and pray together.

KEY   ⦿ Informal   🎛 Formal   ☁ Reflective   👥 All-age friendly   ♡ Favour

Offering of Items

YOU WILL NEED *The items that people brought in for today (see page 31)*

Ask the congregation to reflect on what it might mean to offer the work of their hands as worship to God. Invite them to look at the item that they have brought in, and to ask God to reveal how they might glorify him in its use.

Place an altar table in a central position, and invite the congregation to lay down their items temporarily on the table as a symbol of offering their work to God as worship. Reassure everyone that this is a symbolic act, and that they will be able to get their item back at the end of the activity! This works well during a time of sung worship.

Once the congregation has offered their items, return them. If you have a small congregation, you might be able to pick up an item from the table, for example a laptop, then return it to the owner, saying something like, "Here is your laptop: use it to glorify and serve the Lord." Alternatively, everyone could collect their item then speak similar sending words to each other in pairs.

Heading Out

YOU WILL NEED *A sign (15 minutes preparation)*

Some churches have a sign above the door as you go in which says 'You are now entering a place of worship.' The idea of this activity is to introduce a sign which people see as they go out of the building, perhaps above the door on the inside, saying the same thing. Use this as an opportunity to remind the congregation that the 'outside' is as much a place of worship as within the church building. You could tie this in with singing the song 'I will worship' or similar as you leave the worship time.

Sending Prayer – Prepare the Way

This prayer is based on a prophesy of Isaiah, which is applied to John the Baptist. It reflects on how this relates to us today, and how we will be sent into the different parts of our lives, acting and speaking in ways that bring glory to God.

All: **Prepare the way of the Lord:**
Leader: Make his paths straight,
bringing honour to his name.
Prepare the way of the Lord:
With courage and kindness,
honesty and hope.
Prepare the way of the Lord:
With much strength or little,
whatever you have.

Prepare the way of the Lord:
With a smile, a helping hand,
and a listening ear.
Prepare the way of the Lord:
With words of vision and encouragement,
challenge and direction.
Prepare the way of the Lord:
With acts of compassion,
and generous hearts.

Prepare the way of the Lord:
For the young, the old, and all in between.
Prepare the way of the Lord:
Though the world seems against you,
and the road may be hard.
Prepare the way of the Lord:
Make his paths straight,
bringing honour to his name.
Prepare the way of the Lord.

© **Dave Hopwood, used with permission**

Song Suggestions

Gathering

As we gather (Whatever we do) by Joel Payne – *modern song*
All of life is worship

Lord, as the day begins by Timothy Dudley-Smith – *traditional hymn*
Committing a work day to God

Praise

In the light of your mercy ♡ ▣ **by Sam Hargreaves** – *all-age song*
Offering our whole life to God

God in my living (Everything) by Tim Hughes – *modern song*
God in all of life

O God beyond all praising by Michael Parry – *traditional hymn*
Hymn rooted in our everyday experiences, and
committing our lives to a 'sacrifice of praise'

Response

Before you I kneel (A Worker's Prayer) ♡ **by Keith Getty, Kristyn Getty,
Stuart Townend, Jeff Taylor** – *modern hymn*
Offering the work we do in our daily lives

I will offer up my life by Matt Redman – *modern song*
Responding in giving of ourselves

Take my life and let it be by Frances Ridley Havergal – *traditional hymn*
Unpacking the different things we offer back to God, including the work of our hands

Will you come and follow me (The Summons) by John L Bell – *celtic song*
Call of God for us to follow in every sphere

Sending

Christ be in my waking by Stuart Townend, Simon Brading – *modern hymn*
Whole life for Jesus

From heaven you came (The Servant King) by Graham Kendrick – *modern
hymn*
Following Jesus' example of service in everyday life

Father, help your people by Fred Kaan – *traditional hymn*
Asking God to help us work in a Christ-like way

KEY Informal Formal Reflective 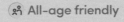 All-age friendly Favouri

Notes

week 4
WORSHIPPING INSPIRES OUR EVERYDAY SPEECH

Key passage: James 5:13–18

Whatever your tradition, there will be important words within your worship life. Liturgies, songs and prayers repeat and emphasise certain phrases. What words are used regularly in your gatherings? How are they shaping your congregation for whole lives of worship?

This week explores how the words of our worship shape us to speak in the world. Together we learn new language that gives us a bigger sense of who God is and how he is involved with our everyday lives. But along with language, we learn new responses. In a world of grumbling, we learn to dig out the blessings and give thanks for them. In a world that reacts to suffering with despair or cynicism, we learn words of lament that are rooted in hope. In a world where we fear the stranger, we learn to greet others in the name of Jesus and find that they become our sister or brother. All this helps us to see the world differently, and to speak and pray in line with God's heart.

We have included activities that help your congregation speak and pray about what is going on in their lives beyond the church walls. Encourage everyone to come to God, however they are feeling and whatever their mistakes or triumphs, with confidence that God hears their fragile words and acts upon them.

> Video four: A reminder of the power of words in all their range and pitch

KEY ⣿ Informal   ⣿ Formal   ⟲ Reflective   ⚇ All-age friendly   ♡ Favour

Gathering

Invitation 1 MIN

God listens.
He is a God who hears our cry.
He is a God who turns his face towards us,
who gives us his full attention.

Today, he invites you to speak.
If you're in trouble – to pray.
If you're happy – to praise him.
If you're ill – to ask for help.
If you're guilty – to confess.

The prayer of a righteous person is powerful
and effective.
Let us turn to the God who hears.

Amen.

Sharing the Peace 5 MIN

Our words are not only directed to God – we can
build one another up with how we speak. Paul
wrote to the Thessalonian church: 'encourage one
another and build each other up' (1 Thessalonians
5:11). If we learn to do this in the context of church
worship, we can take it out to the people we meet
on our frontlines. Take the opportunity to make use
of the 'peace-sharing' time traditionally associated
with communion to greet one another with a word
of appreciation or affirmation. If it helps, invite
people to encourage the person they are greeting.
For example

> 'I am grateful for how you _____,'
> 'Something I like about you is _____,'
> 'God is using you in _____,'
> 'You encourage me'
> 'God loves you'
> 'You are a vital part of this church'.

Blessed Be Your Name
 5 MIN

YOU WILL NEED *Screen to show the PowerPoint*

The PowerPoint has four images which relate to Matt
and Beth Redman's song. Ask people to consider
which image resonates with them as they come to
worship today. Then say the words together.

Leader: We say together:
All: **If you're splashing in streams of**
abundance,
we welcome you – share your joy.
If you're parched in a desert wasteland,
we welcome you – share your doubts.
If you're relaxing in the light of contentment,
we welcome you – share your peace.
If you're stumbling on a road of suffering,
we welcome you – share your pain.

We pray together:
God of water, earth, light and brokenness
we welcome you, as you welcome us.

Amen.

Favourite Lines 5 MIN

YOU WILL NEED *Small pieces of paper and pens,*
or one large sheet, or a mobile phone

Invite people to share a line from a prayer, song
or the Bible which has been helpful to them. You
could ask people to write these on small pieces of
paper, hand them in, and then redistribute them
among the congregation as random encouragements.
Alternatively, people could write their lines up on a
huge sheet of paper, or text them to a central phone
number to be displayed digitally.

 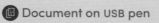

Prayer & Bible

Lord's Prayer 2 MIN

If you say the Lord's Prayer regularly in church, people can become numb to its radical implications. It can be helpful, before you say it, to remind the congregation of how this prayer can transform the way we look at the whole of life.

For example, you can point out that every time we ask for God's Kingdom to come on earth, we are saying that we are not happy with the existing status quo. We are declaring that we have a different vision of what the world should be like. This goes a long way beyond vague hope or despair about how things are – we are calling God's reality down to our everyday existence.

Think about how you might introduce this prayer to point people outwards beyond the church walls.

Intercession for the Frontline 15 MIN

This activity facilitates a time of intercession for four or five situations in the world and on your congregation's frontlines. You might like to prepare a selection of images from your local area and display these as you pray.

1 Pray for each of the five situations, leaving silence for people to respond in their hearts. If you have a PowerPoint prepared, display the images.
2 End each section by saying 'The prayer of a righteous person is powerful and effective.'
3 Invite the congregation to respond: **'Lord have mercy'**.

If you want to do this musically, you could have quiet music playing underneath the prayers. The congregation could sing the 'Lord have mercy' or the Greek *'Kyrie Eleison'* as their response. There are a number of settings listed in the songs at the end of the session.

Frontline Prayer
 3 MIN

YOU WILL NEED *Words projected or printed*

The words of the Lord's Prayer are powerful and formative, but sometimes they can become so familiar that we fail to make the connections with our everyday lives. Here the congregation and leader make those connections together.

All: **Our Father in heaven,
hallowed be your name.**
Leader: We give you the glory, as Lord over every part of our lives.
Your Kingdom come, your will be done, on earth as it is in heaven.
May your Kingdom come in our work places and our homes, may your will be done in the places where we live our lives, on earth as it is in heaven.
Give us today our daily bread,
You are our true provider. Remind us of this as we work, cook, care and share.
**And forgive us our sins,
as we forgive those who sin against us.**
We confess our everyday mistakes and failures. Help us to act towards the people we meet on our frontlines in the same gracious way you act towards us.
**Lead us not into temptation,
but deliver us from evil.**
Guide us, Holy Spirit, in the places we find ourselves, to walk in your ways and act in your will.
For the Kingdom, the power, and the glory are yours,
This is all about you. We submit our frontlines, our ambitions, our lives to your will, as offerings of worship.
now and forever,

Amen.

 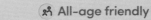

James 5:13–18
Prayer 3 MIN

These are formal prayers of intercession. They connect with the passage and with the idea that our words are powerful, bringing about change in the world because of the power of God's Word (Hebrews 4:12).

Leader: James wrote to the early church: 'Is anyone among you in trouble? Let them pray.' We think about our own troubles, and the troubles in the world around us. We speak peace to conflict situations. We speak wholeness into broken lives. We speak abundance into places of famine and drought. Help us to remember that our words are powerful,
All: **because your Word is powerful, sharper than a double-edged sword.**

James also wrote: 'Is anyone happy? Let them sing songs of praise.' We thank you, God, for the blessings in our own lives, and for your provision across the world. May our gratitude turn to words of worship to you, wherever we find ourselves. Help us to remember that our words are powerful, **because your Word is powerful, sharper than a double-edged sword.**

James encouraged his churches: 'Is anyone among you sick? Let them call the elders of the church to pray over them...' We pray healing for those in our church who are ill. Make us bold to pray for people we meet in our everyday lives. And please give us grace and peace for situations where our prayers are not answered the way we immediately expect. Help us to remember that our words are powerful, **because your Word is powerful, sharper than a double-edged sword, Amen.**

Go Ahead and Speak to God: James 5:13–18

2 MIN

YOU WILL NEED *Quiet background music*

This is an adapted, interactive Bible reading, which any age or ability can participate in.

Leader: Are you in trouble?
All: **Go ahead and speak to God!**
Go ahead and pray.

Are you happy?
Go ahead and speak to God!
Go ahead, sing songs of praise.

Are you ill?
Go ahead and speak to God!
Call friends over to pray for you.

Do you have faith?
Go ahead and speak to God!
He will make you well.

Have you done wrong?
Go ahead and speak to God!
He will forgive you.

Do you have brothers and sisters in Christ?
Go ahead and speak to God!
Speak to God for each other.

Elijah was a human being, just like you and me. He went ahead and spoke to God, asking for it not to rain. It did not rain for three and a half years! Then, he went ahead and spoke to God and it started raining again, and the plants started growing again. So, whatever is going on in our lives, what should we do?
Go ahead and speak to God!

Sermon

Core Message: Our words matter, and the words of our worship shape us to speak in the world.

Key passage: James 5:13–18

All the words we have used today in our worship have been significant. They shape us for life in the wider world. Together we gain a bigger sense of who God is and how he is involved with our everyday lives. In a world of grumbling, we learn to dig out the blessings and give thanks for them. In a world that reacts to suffering with despair or cynicism, we learn words of lament that are rooted in hope. In a world where we fear the stranger, we learn to greet others in the name of Jesus and find that they become our sister or brother.

It's not surprising, then, that God challenges us to pay attention to our words and speech. In his letter, James builds on and applies teaching found in books like Proverbs and the gospels which emphasises a close link between our words and our hearts (cf. Proverbs 15:28, Luke 6:45). Our words reveal something of what is in our hearts. And words have power to change our hearts too – just think of prayer, or the words of a good friend. So out of his rich store of wisdom, James reminds us that

1   **All seasons of life are included**

Our worship includes times of trouble or sickness, times of happiness and sadness. James encourages his congregations to bring all situations before God not only because he knows that God hears and responds, but because they're also learning a new way of responding. The words we sing and pray and speak to one another on Sunday give us a vocabulary to speak to God and other people in all the varied circumstances of Monday to Saturday life. Words used in gathered worship equip us for scattered life. When something goes well at work, we don't just take the credit all for ourselves, we can thank God. When we are saddened by something on the news, we don't just despair, we pray for God's mercy. When we are feeling powerless on our frontline, we don't just give up, we pray for the Spirit to fill us again.

2   **Everyone is included**

It must have been so encouraging to hear that everyone had a part in helping one another. James had a vision of the church where the poor were given dignity (1:9; 2:1–4) and where the rich were made aware of the particular temptations that their situation could provoke (1:10–11; 4:13–5:6). They were a community dependent on one another. So during our worship when we pray for one another, when we rejoice with one another, when we confess our failures to one another, we use our words not only to support each other, but to create a different kind of community and a different way of life. Words in gathered worship form us to make a difference in the whole of our lives.

3   **Words are directed to God who hears and acts**

God is an active partner in our gatherings. Our worship is for God, our prayers are to God, and our thanksgiving is because of God. And he acts. These words are powerful because God hears them, and he acts on them – when we're together and when we're apart. The example James uses is of Elijah. Elijah brought his words before God about the situation that people were facing as a nation. He was human just like us, frail and flawed. But God heard his prayers and acted on them, with remarkable results.

Do we need to take more risks with our words in church and outside church? Do we need to learn to pray more boldly and speak up for God's Kingdom? What might God do if we did?

Response & Sending

How Will I Speak? ☁ 📖 ⏱ 5–8 MIN

YOU WILL NEED *Prayer points prepared as described below, music*

This is a guided meditation to help people think through different situations in the week, and reflect on how they will speak in response. Encourage people to be open to the Holy Spirit as you read.

> Father God, Thank you that you are always present with us,
> thank you that you are interested in every aspect of our lives.
> Reveal to us now truth and wisdom about the words we speak.
> In Jesus' name, Amen.
>
> Imagine the place where you interact with others the most during the week; it could be your workplace, with family in the home or at some other meeting place. Imagine what you can see in that place, what sounds you can hear and what it feels like to be there.
>
> Now, imagine the people you interact with in that place. Imagine their faces, their eyes, their personalities. What do you feel when you think of these people? Do you feel love? A sense of anxiety? Or perhaps you feel neutral towards them?
>
> Now imagine a typical interaction you may have with these people. Pay careful attention to what you might say to them. Which words do you speak? How do you speak these words?
>
> Now hold the words up to an imaginary magnifying glass and reflect on them in God's presence.
>
> How do the words reflect on the hope of Christ within you?
> How do the words reflect on the Father's love for you and for the person you speak to?
> Ask God to reveal to you the power of your words.
>
> Now turn your reflection into prayer. We will all feel drawn to different responses. Perhaps you feel the need to confess and seek forgiveness. Perhaps you want to intercede for the people you interact with. Perhaps you experience a sense of thankfulness and you want to turn to God in praise. Whatever your experience, turn to God in response.
>
> *PAUSE*
>
> Father God, we bring all these thoughts and reflections to you.
> Thank you for what you have spoken and revealed to us.
> Please help us to bring glory to you wherever we find ourselves.
> In Jesus' name, Amen.

 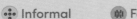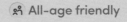

Worship Words 💙 ⠿ 🖥 🕐 10 MIN

YOU WILL NEED *Printed cards and posters for each word*

Put up posters with five phrases around the church: 'Hallelujah', 'Lord, Have Mercy', 'How Long, O Lord', 'Thank You, God', 'Come, Holy Spirit'. Ask people to choose one phrase which they want to learn to use more often in their everyday lives, and to go to that poster. Here they can pick up a card to encourage and remind them of their response. Give people the opportunity to talk about the cards, and possibly pray for one another in small groups at the station. Cards to encourage can be printed from the USB pen.

Sacrifice of Praise

YOU WILL NEED *Words projected or printed*

This is a prayer based on Hebrews 13:15–16. It sends the congregation out to be living sacrifices in all we do, specifically including the 'fruit of our lips'.

All: **Let us offer a sacrifice of praise:**
Leader: a sacrifice through Jesus.

Let us offer a sacrifice of praise:
a continual offering.

Let us offer a sacrifice of praise:
the fruit of lips that confess Christ's name.

Let us offer a sacrifice of praise:
doing good and sharing with others.

Let us offer a sacrifice of praise:
for with such sacrifices God is pleased.

Amen.

Blessing ▥ 🖥 🕐 2 MIN

This blessing prayer, based on Philippians 1:3–11, emphasises the importance of words. This works well read together as a whole congregation.

May you find joy in each other.
May you find gospel partnerships in each other.
May he who began a good work in you
carry it on to completion until the day of
Christ Jesus.

May you carry each other in your hearts,
and share God's grace with each other.
May you have the affection of Jesus Christ
for each other.

May your love abound more and more,
in knowledge and depth of insight,
so that you may be able to discern what is best
and may be pure and blameless for the day of Christ,
filled with the fruit of righteousness that
comes through Jesus Christ – to the glory
and praise of God.

Amen.

Song Suggestions

Gathering

Everybody's welcome by Nigel Hemming – *all-age song*
Emphasising God's welcome

Come you thankful by Sam Hargreaves – *all-age song*
Joyful song reminding us that we can come as we are, diverse people united in Christ

Blessed be your name by Matt Redman, Beth Redman – *modern song*
Acknowledging the different phases of life when God is still worthy of our worship

Praise

Our Father by Marcus Meier – *modern song*
Based on the Lord's Prayer

Abana in heaven (Arabic Lord's Prayer) by Laila Constantine, adapted by Greg Scheer – *Middle-Eastern style*
Egyptian version of the Lord's Prayer, translated into English

Our Father in heaven by Eric Wyse – *traditional hymn*
Traditional setting of the Lord's Prayer

Prayer & Bible

We call to you ♡ **by Caroline Bonnett, Sue Rinaldi** – *intercessory song*
Refrain 'Lord have mercy'

Kyrie eleison (Traditional Russian Orthodox) – *chant style*
Two settings, one from the Russian Orthodox church and one from Ghana

O Lord hear my prayer by Jacques Berthier (Taizé) – *chant style*
Intercessory song, simple and repeated

Speak, O Lord by Keith Getty, Stuart Townend – *modern hymn*
Focusing on God's word to us

Sending

Forth in your name by Graham Kendrick based on Charles Wesley – *modernised hymn*
Being sent out to worship

We are called to be God's people ♡ **by Thomas A. Jackson** – *traditional hymn*
Our calling to live for God, speaking out for truth and justice

Take my life and let it be by Frances Ridley Havergal – *traditional hymn*
Unpacking the different things we offer back to God (includes lips)

 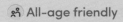

Notes

week 5

WORSHIPPING FOCUSES OUR WAVERING HEARTS

Key passage: Revelation 2:1–7

This week looks again at our motivations for worship. God is not looking for a people who are 'going through the motions' in worship, but a people who are loving him, one another and the world around them.

We began the series reminding ourselves that worship was rooted in the gospel and we end by reminding ourselves that love should be the foundation for all our actions and intentions. It's easy to find ourselves slipping into an attitude that says, 'Of course we love God, and other people and the world around us, but we are busy. We need to get things done.' Love gets lost in the maelstrom of life.

This session refocuses us on the God who is love and reminds us that all our worship is a response to what he has done first for us in sending Jesus. Our wavering hearts are refocused and our capacity to love grows.

This session includes a number of ways to approach communion, that wonderful invitation to a table which reminds us that God so loved the world that he sent his son for us.

 Video five: The faithfulness
of the God whom we worship

KEY   ⋮⋮⋮ Informal   ▥ Formal   ◌ Reflective   ⚥ All-age friendly   ♡ Favou

Gathering

Invitation   1 MIN

It started with God.
He had the first word.
In the beginning, he was.

He started, we followed.
He initiated, we responded.
He invited, we answered.
He loved.

First of all, he loved.
He loved us first,
so that we could love.
Let us respond in worship.

Amen.

Enter God's Love   8 MIN

YOU WILL NEED *A ball of red yarn*

This works best for a small to medium gathering. In a larger church you could adapt it into a group activity.

1 Invite the group to form a circle.
2 The leader starts by reading 1 John 3:1:
   'See what great love the Father has lavished on us, that we should be called children of God!'
3 Ask the group to pass the ball of yarn along to the next person in the circle, with the first person holding on to one end, while speaking the words:
   'Welcome, you are a loved child of God!'
4 The group should continue to repeat these words, while passing the ball of yarn to each person, allowing it to unravel and each holding on to the yarn.
5 When the circle is complete, ask everyone to move themselves into the circle of yarn, lifting the yarn over their heads. There might be laughter and tangles at this point!
6 Once everyone is inside, pray the following prayer: *'Father, thank you for including us in your great family. Thank you that we are your children, surrounded by your love. Thank you that you welcome us into your love today. Help us to respond to your love in worship. Amen.'*

'BECAUSE THE GOD CHRISTIANS ADORE IS ENGAGED IN THE WORLD, ADORATION OF GOD LEADS TO ACTION IN THE WORLD AND ACTION IN THE WORLD LEADS TO ADORATION OF GOD.'

— **Miroslav Volf,** *Worship: Adoration and Action*

Praise, Prayer & Bible

One in Christ 👥 🖥 📖 🕐 3 MIN

This prayer/poem helps us to reflect on both our differences and our unity in Jesus. Love for one another is likely to be part of the 'first love' mentioned in the passage, so it is good to highlight this at the beginning of the service. All-age friendly, this prayer can be made more multi-sensory by including sign language for the response part:

- **We** – right hand, palm up, sweep from left hand towards the right side of the body
- **One** – hold up right index finger
- **Christ** – right index finger pointing in left palm, followed by left index finger pointing in right palm

Leader: We are many,
God's great diversity,
All: **yet we are one in Christ.**

Different faces,
different races,
yet we are one in Christ.

Butchers, bakers,
website makers,
bankers, tailors,
teachers, sailors,
yet we are one in Christ.

Fathers, mothers,
sisters, brothers,
single, married,
broken, carried,
yet we are one in Christ.

The happy, the clappy,
the barely out of nappies,
the ancient, the modern,
the famous, the forgotten,
yet we are one in Christ.

Some hopeful, some hopeless,
some cope well, some cope less.
Some sure and some doubt,
some whisper, some shout,
yet we are one in Christ.

Those with abundance,
those with need,
those who are generous
or wrestle with greed,
yet we are one in Christ.

Elbows, tummies, knees and noses,
kidneys, femurs, teeth and toeses.
Some unmentionable, some protected,
some accepted, some rejected,
yet we are one in Christ.

A broken body,
torn apart,
mars God's image,
breaks God's heart.
And yet our Father knows how the end will be,
when all his kids will sing in harmony,
the bride will dazzle, her branches bloom,
so add your voice to hymn the tune
that we are one in Christ.

Psalm 96 Praise Shout 👥 🖥 📖 🕐 2 MIN

This is a praise shout, paraphrasing Psalm 96, that works well read together. It encourages heartfelt praise, so encourage people to give it their all.

Sing it out!
Sing the Lord a new song. Sing it out!
Sing out, all the earth. Sing it out!
Bless his name forever. Sing it out!
For day by day, he saves.

Tell every nation his glorious deeds,
every people his marvellous works.
Praise him, for praise his greatness deserves,
his greatness above all gods.

For the gods of the peoples are idols.
They're idle!
And nothing can come from their hands.
But the Lord made the heavens, he reigns as our king,
and in power and beauty he stands.

So write it down!
Every nation, every people. Write it down!
God is glorious and strong. Write it down!
For his name deserves all glory. Write it down!
Bring him offerings and praise.

Then worship the Lord, in his splendour and holiness,
and tremble before him, earth.
And tell every nation, 'The Lord is king,
justice firm as the earth he formed.'
And heavens, be happy. Rocks rejoice.
Seas shout, and sea creatures, too.
Fields wave, and field mice join in the song,
as the forests find voice and sing.

Then sing it out!
For the Lord is coming.
Sing it out!
Coming to judge the earth.
Sing it out!
His judgements will be righteous. Sing it out!
His judgements will be true.

© **Bob Hartman, used with permission**

Giving Thanks 👥 🕐 8 MIN

YOU WILL NEED *Musicians to lead a song, perhaps a wireless microphone*

This activity gets us thinking about how God loves his people and provides for us, encouraging us to respond with thanks and praise.

1 Ask people to bring to mind one way in which they have known God's love and faithfulness over the last week – it could be something big like a new job, something smaller like seeing a sunrise, or anything in between.
2 Keeping these thoughts in mind, sing a song which focuses on giving thanks for God's love and care. Two are listed at the end of this session, for example *Give thanks (Great is the Lord)*.
3 Once you have sung the song, keep the music going quietly and invite some people to take it in turns to share their thoughts.
4 The wider congregation can respond by singing a short refrain from the song: *His love endures forever*, or *Give thanks to the Lord*. Allow time for all the people who want to share, and then close with a final chorus.

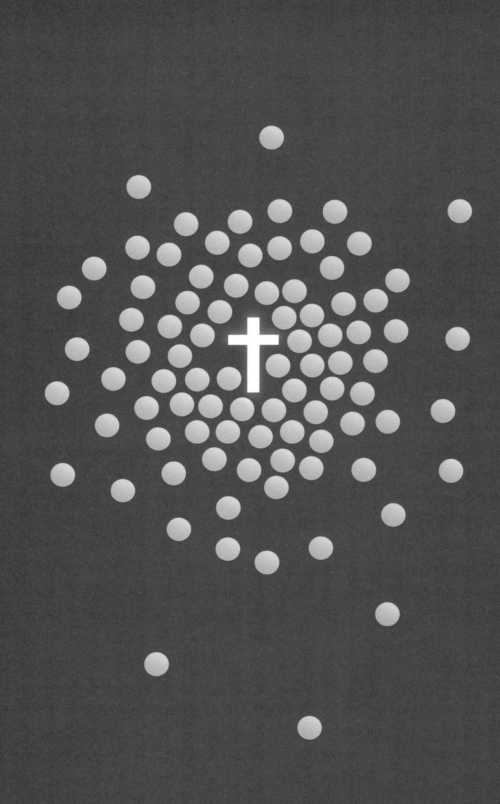

Sermon

Core Message: Worship is empty without God transforming our hearts.

Key passage: Revelation 2:1–7

You can look like you are getting things so right. Yet you can be so wrong. This is certainly true in the Christian life and in worship as well. Worship can inadvertently become about musical technique, or liturgy, or delivering a professional performance. It's too easy to concentrate on the wrong things.

For Christians in the Roman empire, life was stressful. They were marginalised and persecuted, yet somehow they kept going. They stayed faithful, put up with the hardships and worked hard to please God. This was the church in Ephesus. And yet they had forgotten that it was all about love. They had abandoned their first love (Revelation 2:4). It's not clear who they had stopped loving. It could have been God, it could have been one another within the church, it could have been their neighbours out in the world. It could have been all three. In fact, all three seems most likely, because loving God and loving neighbour tend to go hand in hand (Mark 12:33, 1 John 4:21).

They were called back to their love relationships. This seems to be a common complaint for God's people in the Old Testament (Amos 5:21–24, Micah 6:6–8) and the New Testament (1 Corinthians 13:1–3).

How do we keep love at the heart of our worship?

1 **Rooted in God's love**

   It begins by recognising that our worship is fuelled by an awareness of God's love for us. God loves us first, he has freed us from sins, and has made us to be a kingdom of priests – to serve him and his purposes (Revelation 1:5–6). When we forget this, we can come back to him in repentance (Revelation 2:5), and receive his love and acceptance afresh.

2 **Loving one another**

   When we know that we are loved, and that we didn't deserve that love, we are able to be recreated as a worshipping people. This gets worked out in our relationships with other believers. Of course we are all different and will have disagreements, but we are called to be reconciled as we come to worship (Matthew 5:23–24).

3 **Sent out to love**

   Finally, the love we have found in God and developed among our brothers and sisters gets worked out as we relate to people on our frontlines. The church in Ephesus received a letter outlining just how God was at work in their world. They would be reminded of the hope that was theirs, and that would mean they could live out the new life of the Kingdom, even in the darkest places.

'FAR FROM BEING A RETREAT FROM THE REAL WORLD, WORSHIP ENABLES CHRISTIANS TO SEE WHAT THE REAL WORLD IS AND EQUIPS THEM TO LIVE IN IT.'

— **Rodney Clapp,** *A Peculiar People*

Response & Sending

Praise the Lord   2 MIN

YOU WILL NEED *Words projected or printed*

This riff on Psalm 149 sums up a lot of the themes in this series, and sends the congregation out to worship and love in all the places they find themselves.

All: **PRAISE THE LORD!**
Leader: Praise him in the streets and the city.
Praise him in the towns and the villages.
Praise him in the pubs and the churches,
in the sports stadiums and back gardens.
PRAISE THE LORD!

Praise him in the lounge
and the kitchen,
in the bathroom and the hallway.
Praise him when the sun shines
and when the rain falls.
Praise him with a smile and with tears,
in the mountains and the valleys
and the plains in between.
PRAISE THE LORD!

Praise him with your own voice,
in your own way.
Praise him with half a breath
or a lungful of shouting,
sitting still or running a marathon.
PRAISE THE LORD!

Praise him with a simple
lifting of your eyes,
or with an ear-splitting roar,
with a shout of praise or a cry of anguish,
with a whispered plea or a gentle smile.
PRAISE THE LORD!

Praise him with words,
thoughts, songs and actions,
in your work, leisure, competition,
kindness, service and sacrifices.
Praise him with the small things and the great.
PRAISE THE LORD!

Praise him as you help others.
Praise him in those unseen things you do.
Praise him as you do what you do best,
and by doing the difficult things:
PRAISE THE LORD!

© Dave Hopwood, used with permission

Practical Acts of Love
 10 MIN

YOU WILL NEED *Simple gifts to give away*

We have heard in the sermon that, just as we received God's love, so we are called to share it out on our frontlines. Give your congregation an easy way to show love in the week. Hand out small gifts such as chocolate bars, and challenge the congregation to think of one person on their frontline who is not a Christian and could use love and encouragement. Invite them to give their chocolate or other gift to that person as a sign of love. You could get people to share in small groups the person who has come to mind, and to pray for each other in those groups. You could then sing a song such as 'Bring heaven to earth, Lord' or 'Shine'. Consider following up this idea the next week, to see if there are stories of how people got on.

You could end this series with the act of worship given to us by Jesus himself – bread and wine. As you introduce the sacrament you can emphasise some of the themes of this week, for example drawing attention to God's love shown through Christ's sacrifice on the cross (1 John 4:10).

Receiving God's Love

 10 MIN

The PowerPoint has verses which remind us of the truth of God's love for us. Sometimes we need to actively remember and receive this love. As people come to take communion, you might like to create a space with silence or quiet instrumental music while the slides cycle around, and people can receive God's love afresh.

Taken, Blessed, Broken & Given 10 MIN

Alternatively, you might like to use Henri Nouwen's image of being Taken, Blessed, Broken and Given (see his book *Life of the Beloved* (Hodder & Stoughton, 2016)). Just as Jesus took the bread, blessed it, broke it and gave it, so we too are chosen by God, blessed, broken and yet sent out to be gifts to the world. Invite people to reflect on which of these images relates to them the most at the present time, and how God is sending each of us out to our frontlines in this way.

Handwashing & Communion 15 MIN

YOU WILL NEED *Basins with warm water, towels, seats*

Handwashing represents a counter-cultural act of love, rooted in the actions of Jesus. You could read John 13:1–17, and/or use the song 'All the room was hushed and still' to introduce a time of washing each other's hands. Speak about how this is a practical way of showing love and service to one another.

Loving Hands 6 MIN

Explain that you are going to engage in a reflection and an act of sending using our hands. Leave a moment's pause between each paragraph for the congregation to consider their personal response. If you are leading this with small children present, allow for time in the pauses to verbalise together as families what we might imagine.

Leader: First, I invite you to hold both hands out as if you are receiving a gift. Consider all the gifts that God has given you – the things you can do and are good at. The material gifts and provisions. Imagine that all those things are in your hands.

Next, form your hands into a heart by touching palms and finger nails together. Consider the love that God has shown you. He sent Jesus to die for your sins and he welcomed you as one of his children. Imagine that all this love is in your hands.

Finally, open your hands up, palm upwards and stretch your arms forwards as if giving something to someone. Draw to mind the gifts you imagined were in your hands. Draw to mind God's love that you imagined was in your hands. As God sends you from here, ask him to reveal to you how you can share these gifts and this love with someone. Let's pray:

All: **Father God,
Send us out
to love you
to receive your love
and to share that love with the world.
In the name of Christ,**

Amen.

Song Suggestions

Praise

Give thanks to the Lord (forever) by Chris Tomlin – *modern song*
Gratitude, with refrain 'His love endures forever'

Give thanks (Great is the Lord) by Sam Hargreaves – *modern song*
Gratitude, with refrain 'Give thanks to the Lord'

Your love is amazing by Brenton Brown, Brian Doerksen – *modern song*
Joy at God's love for us

Higher than the mountains by Brian Johnson, Christa Black Gifford, Jeremy Riddle – *modern song*
God's love is bigger than our problems

My first love by Stuart Townend – *Celtic style*
Upbeat song about our love for God

Response

When the music fades by Matt Redman – *modern song*
Encouragement to come back to the 'heart of worship'

I love you Lord by Laurie Klein – *modern song*
Simple chorus expressing love for God

All the room was hushed and still (Love each other) by Graham Kendrick – *story song*
The foot washing story, encouraging us to love one another

Bring heaven to earth, Lord (We are blessed) by Andy Flannagan – *modern song*
Committing ourselves to go and love people out
beyond the church walls in the ways we live

Shine by Nick Jackson – *all-age song*
Upbeat song, committing ourselves to shine for God in the
world and show the love he has poured out on us

Communion

Here is love by William Rees, tran. William Edwards – *traditional hymn*
Focusing on the love of God shown on the cross

Here is bread by Mark Bradford – *modern song*
Telling of communion as the place where we see God's love
and grace, for the restoration of the whole world

Sending

I love you Lord (Joy) by John Ellis – *modern song*
Connecting love for God with shining our light in the world

When I survey the wondrous cross ♡ **by Isaac Watts** – *traditional hymn*
The cross as the expression of God's love – leading us to bring our whole lives

Come set your rule and reign (Build your Kingdom) ♡
by Rend Collective – *modern song*
Calling out to God to transform the world and our local area through us

We are called to be God's people by Thomas A. Jackson – *traditional hymn*
Our calling to live for God, showing his love and acting in the world for him

Notes

Journeying on in worship

So what happens next?

Our hope is that these ideas and perspectives have inspired you. We trust that you're convinced that how you think and pray and prepare for gathered worship does make a significant difference to your congregation, Monday to Saturday.

We trust you've had opportunity to experiment and had encouraging feedback. We hope this pack has been helpful in strengthening the connections between gathered and scattered church life.

Perhaps your community has gained a fresh glimpse of God's majesty; has been gripped by the love and power revealed in the life, death and resurrection of Jesus; has opened up further to the infilling of the creative Holy Spirit and has helped one another to see how this changes our perspective on the whole of life. And if that has happened, at least in part, you may be thinking: what next?

Of course, there may be ideas in this pack that you've not yet tried but noted along the way. You can go back to the book *Whole Life Worship* too, and rediscover perspectives and practices to further deepen your gathered worship experience. You can explore websites, such as engageworship.org. All this will be helpful.

But there is more. And the 'more' is not primarily about introducing new ideas. It's about nurturing your own curiosity in people's everyday lives.

Nothing will contribute more to shaping a whole-life culture than developing an understanding of the texture of people's lives Monday to Saturday, finding out what's going on, asking them what God is doing. It is this genuine concern that will generate the creativity that will nurture and sustain a dynamic, healthy relationship between the gathered church and the scattered church, and shape a culture where everyone understands that the whole earth and their whole lives are the Lord's. It is this personal interest that will fuel worship that helps us to live fruitfully and play our part in God's mission – wherever we are.

As Mark Greene put it

> 'The UK will never be reached until we create open, authentic, learning and praying communities that are focused on making whole life disciples who live and share the gospel wherever they relate to people in their daily lives.'

It's a challenging task. And LICC would love to serve you in this. We offer a range of resources, training days, learning hubs, encouragement and support for leaders who are creating whole life disciple-making churches. Our website can guide you through these, or just get in touch.

What opportunities lie ahead for us here! Let's journey on together.